AF796560

MAKE YOUR MONEY WORK

Six Easy Steps to Drive Performance Through Financial Education

By: Travis W. Freeman, CFP®

INFINITY PUBLISHING

ISBN 978-0-7414-7557-2

Printed in the United States of America

Published November 2012

INFINITY PUBLISHING

Toll-free (877) BUY BOOK
Local Phone (610) 941-9999
Fax (610) 941-9959
Info@buybooksontheweb.com
www.buybooksontheweb.com

Dedication

This book is dedicated to my family
to whom I owe everything in my life.

TABLE OF CONTENTS

CHAPTER 1:

THE ISSUES

> *"An investment in knowledge always pays the best interest."*
>
> – Benjamin Franklin

Our dear friend, Ben Franklin, certainly had it right when he coined this popular quote back in the 18th century. This viewpoint is timeless and remains just as true today. However, given the difficult economic times that began at the turn of the 21st century, I imagine that Mr. Franklin, if he were alive today, would have easily emphasized his message of education for money and personal finance.

It is quite understandable why the average American family would feel frustrated, confused, or distrustful about investments, finance, and money today. Two of the three worst recessions in American history occurred within a short timeframe after the late 1990s. These events have been strong enough to reshape the behaviors and attitudes of the American public with regard to money and personal finance. Let's take a brief stroll down memory lane to relive just a few events that have shaped our recent financial world:

- March 2000 – The "tech" stock market bubble bursts. The NASDAQ index loses more than 10 percent of its value in just 10 days from March 10 (peak) to March 20*.
- November 2001 – The atrocious terrorist attacks of November 11 occur, driving the stock market down 14

percent and stirring speculation about the economy, fiscal policy, and war.

- June 2002 – Tax auditing firm, Arthur Andersen, is indicted on criminal charges for the accounting scandal of Enron. Numerous additional scandals and bankruptcies followed, affecting millions of Americans. Sweeping legislative changes for corporate America came soon after.
- March 2003 – The United States launches an invasion of Iraq, stirring concern about the costs, repercussions, and losses it would cause.
- August 2005 – Hurricane Katrina hits the Southern United States, followed by hurricane Rita, causing $91.2 billion in damage between the two disasters[1,2].
- April 2006 – Median prices for new American homes begin rapid decline after increasing over 83 percent between April 1996 and April 2006[3].
- July 2007 – Countrywide Financial Corporation warns of "difficult conditions" in the housing and mortgage markets. The company nearly declares bankruptcy the very next year before being purchased by Bank of America.
- March 2008 – One of the world's largest investment banking firms, Bear Stearns, is sold to JPMorgan Chase through a rushed weekend deal, brokered in part by government officials. Bear Stearns had started in 1923

---

1 United States Department of Commerce, June 2010. "Hurricane Katrina Service Assessment Report."

2 National Hurricane Center, www.nhc.noaa.gov, June 2007. "Tropical Cyclone Report: Hurricane Rita."

3 US Census, www.census.gov. "Median and Average Sales Prices of New Homes Sold in the United States, Jan. 1963-Oct. 2011. "

* Indices are unmanaged and cannot be invested into directly. Past performance is no guarantee of future results.

surviving many recessions, including the Great Depression.

- June 2009 – Former NASDAQ chairman, Bernard Madoff, is sentenced to 150 years in prison for the ponzi scheme he orchestrated. Madoff's clients lost tens of billions of dollars due to the fraudulent act.
- March 2010 – President Barrack Obama signs the Affordable Care Act into law, initiating one of the largest changes in health care law in American history. The vast scope of changes are too overwhelming for the public to fully understand.
- March 2011 – One of the most powerful earthquakes in modern history strikes Japan, causing in excess of $100 billion in damages and disrupting global trade for much of the developed world according to Eqecat, a catastrophe modeling company.

Even as a financial professional, following the changes in law, health care, fiscal policy, investments, and the stock market are enough to keep me busy full time. Please remember, I also have a degree in finance and economics, I have several state and federal registrations to practice in the finance industry, and I am a board-certified CFP® *professional*. How on earth is the average American family supposed to feel comfortable about their finances if even professionals find it challenging to keep up with so much rapid change?

What the American family needs amongst this uncertainty is a greater understanding of finance-fundamentals, free from the media frenzy that is notorious for distorting the real impact of events. Let's face it, fear sells television, books, magazines, and newspapers. Most major media outlets are great at selling fear, and the marketplace has had no shortage of fuel to drive it. The combination of fear and innocent ignorance is the perfect recipe for poor decisions.

As an example, we can look at a common mistake made by many Americans in the midst of the recession – selling low. The end of 2008 and the first quarter of 2009 were very bad for stock market performance. During these times, headlines such as "no end in sight, when will it end?" and "global crisis" were common at just about every media outlet. From the news coverage, it appeared we were already going through the 2nd Great Depression. This high-intensity, fear-driven "reporting" of the economy caused millions of Americans to completely ignore their own logic and goals. Instead, they waited until the worst had occurred and decided to step out of their investments after losing large amounts of money. After March 9, 2009, the US stock market recovered sharply. Many of those Americans that had "jumped ship" were very late to enter back into their investments because they were unsure as to how long a recovery would actually last. This caused a realization of large losses and a failure to participate in the large gains that followed throughout the rest of 2009. Fear had driven our human minds to do what they are supposed to do – separate us from harm.

Although I have strong feelings about the timely actions of our media sources, financial knowledge issues also stem from timeless sources. I am sure you are familiar with the old saying, "Money is the root of all evil." This is often misquoted from a biblical passage. In the New Testament (1 Timothy 6:10), there is a phrase that reads, "For the love of money is a root of all kinds of evil." Although most of us can recognize the message this passage aims to deliver, I think it is the love of what money brings that leads to either good or evil. After all, money is simply a tool. If that tool is used for the wrong reasons, it will lead to evil. If used for the right reasons, it can lead to great outcomes. For example, money can be used for illegal drugs and to harm others. However, it can also be used to send a grandchild to college or start a charity. The issue is not with money, but with the constant battle between doing good and succumbing to evil. Money happens to be the common ingredient for behaviors that lead to both outcomes. In our modernized society, money is simply a required part of our lifestyle. In turn, it requires care, respect, and skill to deliver the resulting *good* that we desire.

My Story

When I was young, my parents went through a horrible divorce and custody battle that lasted over two years. If you have ever been party to any sort of legal battle, you know how expensive those years can become. I came to know my way around the county courthouse about as well as my own school. Once the ensuing battle was done, my family was torn to pieces, both emotionally and financially. My mother and father each had spent their retirement assets, personal savings, and the college money once set aside for my younger brother and me on attorneys and court costs. In fact, my mother had to shut down her small business to pay off large debts. We were broke and broken.

I will never forget those years we spent leaning on government assistance programs to keep us going. I was teased at school when friends learned I was receiving aid to help pay for my lunches. Little did they know we were also relying on food stamps to help us keep food in the pantry. We were in what my mother called "survival mode." Trust me when I say that powdered milk tastes nothing like the real stuff. Even gifts during the holidays came by way of donation from churches and non-profit groups.

Luckily, those difficult times did not last forever. Through hard work and a bit of luck, each side of my family eventually rebuilt what was lost. At the time, I was too young to understand what was truly going on within my family. However, I did know it had something to do with money. This was the initial spark that started my fascination of understanding money. That spark brought me to study finance in college and then to become a financial professional. Now, I have the amazing opportunity to teach people about money and how it affects their lives.

Why did I share with you my personal story? Take a look at these events and how they surrounded money and financial decisions. Arguments between my parents were often due to money. It took money to go through a divorce. It took tons of money to go through that horrible custody battle. This led my mother to close her business and my father to spend down his life savings. All along the way, poor financial decisions were made, both out of aggravation and innocent ignorance.

Did these examples remind you of anyone you know? I imagine they did. Why? This is life. People go through divorces, lose businesses, become sick, lose family members, lose jobs, and make poor decisions. Everyone has a story. Some stories are more severe than others, but everyone has one. Each and every example listed above is related to money. Whether we like it or not, money is tied to almost everything we do. Even positive topics such as retiring, traveling, giving to charity, and going to college are directly tied to money. Whether we are discussing events that are in our control or events that are out of our control, money is in the picture. When a lack of understanding about money is combined with major events in life, it can lead us to missed goals or even "survival mode" on food stamps.

Not Just Finance 101

As I share these ideas with you, please know that I am not just talking about a basic understanding of money and finance. Sure, I am certainly speaking to the American families that do not know what a mutual fund is, but I am equally speaking to the American families with above-average knowledge in the world of finance. Even for savvy individuals that enjoy monitoring their 401(k) investments and reading articles about personal finance, they still have a need to make better decisions and to monitor all of the rapid changes going on around them.

I often find that people assume intelligent professionals make wise financial decisions and do not need education in the realm of personal finance. Let's give two examples of professions that are regarded as requiring a great deal of intelligence in our society – attorneys and doctors. I have personally met with many attorneys and doctors on the premise of personal finance. Although I do agree that they often possess an above-average understanding of finance due to their cognitive capacities, they are just as susceptible to unwise decisions as anyone else. In fact, some of them are making more poor decisions than a "blue collar" professional. Please remember, these attorneys and doctors commonly have more to deal with than an average American worker. This may mean being a partner of the firm, having insurance risks with a surgical practice, having multiple properties in different states, or wanting to send children through expensive medical schools. All of these areas are complex and require tremendous planning and expertise.

Aside from having more financial concerns, we are all subject to the same human force of procrastination. I have met with a few attorneys who did not have basic estate documents in place such as wills and trusts. As you know, estate planning is a legal area, prepared professionally by attorneys. How is it that an attorney can be without essential legal documents such as a will? It is the same reason a plumber still has a faucet that leaks and a mechanic hasn't fixed that sound coming from his engine yet. It isn't a matter of knowledge any longer; it is a matter of priority. Making wise financial decisions is a combination of knowledge and priority.

Our society as a whole tends to postpone financial goals until they are staring us in the face. In fact, I wish I could take a picture of someone and add 20 years of aging onto their appearance. Then, I would ask them what they believe their future self would tell them to do today. I imagine they would realize that they need to plan for that older person in the picture. However, most people are busy planning for tomorrow or next year, not their 70s.

Our younger generations tend to be the least concerned about planning for a strong financial future. I believe some societal values are to blame. For example, turn on a TV channel that is targeted to your typical 20 or 30- something. You certainly won't see any commercials or programs about money, insurance, or business. Then, take a look at some of the popular magazines that young men and women read. I recently grabbed a few magazines targeted at women. The headlines on the front read, "20 kinky sex tips, lose 10 pounds fast, and Hollywood surgery shockers." It's no wonder why these young people are learning about money the hard way. Again, this is not a question of a person's education; it is a question of a person's priorities.

The Motivated Group & Professional Advice

For those Americans that do have both the desire for knowledge and the desire to make personal finance a priority, we have a new issue. Where do they go for trusted advice? Acording to a 2011 survey by Sun Life Financial US, which polled about 1,450 people, the No. 1 group people go to for financial advice is family. The No. 2 group people go to is friends, followed by financial professionals in third place. The fourth and fifth groups were tied and came in very close to No. 3 – online news and TV news, respectively.

For the Americans that are actually motivated to make better financial decisions and learn more about personal finance, they turn to unlicensed, non-professional resources. This is likely due to the need for an immediate trusted source. It may also be due to the fact that some financial professionals (I only call them professionals because they have licenses) tend to recommend investment products that benefit themselves through large amounts of compensation. This becomes an issue when it is not disclosed and is recommended to someone that may benefit from a comparable product that pays the *professional* less compensation. Most financial professionals are looking out for the client first, not their own wallets. However, it is extremely hard for the public to discover the difference between an independent professional putting the public's interests first and the broker who may legally recommend a certain product over others that pay him or her a larger amount of compensation. Due to this concern, I can understand why many people are hesitant to visit with a licensed professional.

Luckily, there has been progress with changes in law that would further differentiate the two types of professionals listed above – the advisor putting the public's needs first and the broker who isn't legally forced to do so. This is an area that Americans definitely need to understand further. Currently, there are two sets of laws that govern two types of "financial professionals" – investment advisors and brokers. By law, investment advisors must act in a fiduciary capacity and put their clients' needs first, only making recommendations that fit according to that rule. However, brokers only need to make recommendations that are *suitable*. There is a major difference in the verbiage here.

As an example, let's assume you are buying a home and using a real estate professional. You tell this professional that you are looking for a three-bedroom, two-bath home that has a back yard where your young children can play. You tell this person that you want to buy a house somewhere in the greater Chicago area. When this professional takes you to the first home, you walk up to a building that is in need of many structural repairs and is in the worst part of town. However, it does have what you requested – three beds, two baths, and it's in the greater Chicago area. By the way, the real estate professional receives a bigger commission on this property than others because the sellers are willing to pay more to him or her upon purchase.

This was obviously not a recommendation based on your needs. After all, you have young children and need a safe building to call home and a safe neighborhood where they can play. However, this building was, technically, suitable. It had everything you requested. I imagine very few Americans are aware of these different laws that govern financial professionals. Instead, most Americans view all people that say they are "financial professionals" (bankers, brokers, insurance agents, investment advisors, financial planners, wealth managers) as the same. This is one of the major reasons people refrain from visiting with a professional for advice, although doing so would likely yield better results with regard to their goals.

Complexity & Accountability

For those Americans that do understand the differences in laws listed above, yet still rely on non-professional resources for help, they may be able to reach the goals they have; however, it may not be as efficiently as working with a professional. A professional has likely helped hundreds of people work towards financial goals and understands what it takes to achieve them. A professional simply has the skills and knowledge necessary to help you reach those goals more efficiently. A non-professional simply doesn't have the skill set to help someone achieve long-term goals at the same level of efficiency. I believe this reason is twofold. First, let's face it, as life goes on, finance doesn't become less complex, it becomes more complex. You may have a combination of mortgage, retirement, college, long-term care, insurance, tax planning, business, estate, and investment goals requiring your attention. This likely requires financial advisors, CPAs, attorneys, mortgage professionals, etc. The wealthiest people in America certainly didn't become wealthy all on their own; they used the services and advice of professionals along the way, even when they weren't wealthy. Second, a good professional will hold you accountable.

Earlier we discussed the issue of priority with regard to financial goals and knowledge. Accountability ties into that topic. The most common New Year's resolution each and every year is to start exercising and become healthier. Gyms across the country enjoy boosts in memberships each January. However, the gym only experiences those newcomers for the first month or two. Why does this occur? We have lives! There are jobs, kids, home repairs, piano lessons, and personal finances robbing you of your time. However, when someone exercises with a professional trainer, or even with a non-professional that keeps them on track, they are 70 percent more likely to stick to the routine[4].

Exercising isn't complex, but it often requires someone to hold us accountable. This either forces us to begin exercising or helps us achieve our exercise goals more efficiently. A dear friend of mine recently started exercising to improve overall health. He went to the gym regularly and completed his workout routine every time. He told me how glad he was that he forced himself to begin exercising again. To my surprise, about six months later, he hired a personal trainer. After a few weeks he once again told me how great he felt and that he was glad he hired a personal trainer. I asked him why he was glad he hired the personal trainer, and he explained that his workouts were more focused, more intense, and gave him better form. His workouts with a professional were more efficient.

After teaching to groups, I commonly meet people that share their personal stories with me. A woman named Julie once approached me after a speaking program and told me that she felt she was doing just fine with her personal finances and asked me why it may help to her start working with a professional. Julie

---

[4] Livestrong article, "How can a person stay motivated to lose weight if they do not have any motivation at all?" Shannon Marks, June 14, 2011.

knew how hard she had worked at understanding her finances and had seen great improvement over the years. However, what Julie could not see is how much *more* efficient she may be able to become with professional help. There was certainly nothing wrong with what she was doing at the time, but from what she explained, I could see more potential improvement given my professional background.

When my wife and I were shopping for a new home, we looked for many months for that perfect place. We knew what we wanted, but we just couldn't find a place that made us feel like we were at home. Finally, after searching through hundreds of listings and looking through multiple counties, we found a place that we wanted. We asked our agent to put a contract on the home, and we made our first offer. Unfortunately, we were too late. Someone else had already put in a bid that the sellers accepted. We were very disappointed that we had spent months searching for this particular home and now needed to start over again. After a few more weeks of searching, we found another home that we loved. In fact, we both looked at each other when we walked through the front door and said, "This is the place." It was even better than the prior home we wanted. After putting a contract on it that same day, we negotiated with the sellers and eventually sealed the deal.

Looking back, I am so thankful that the contract placed on the first home did not work out. If it had, we never would have found the home with which we fell in love. However, there was certainly nothing wrong with the first home. I'm sure we would have been happy living there. However, we had no idea what was waiting for us just a few weeks later. In Julie's case, there was nothing terribly wrong with her personal finances. She likely would have been fine continuing with her self-made plan. However, she did eventually seek out professional help and was amazed at how much more she learned. More importantly, she admitted that she would have made much more progress if she would have sought professional guidance years ago and was excited about the years to come.

Bringing It All Together

We have covered a number of different topics so far. Let's review what we have covered:

- It is nearly impossible for the average American to fully digest all of the turbulence and change that have occurred in recent years.
- We cannot always rely on the media, as they often inject fear into the veins of major stories and events that affect our financial lives.
- Money is a necessity for almost everything in life and often requires important decision-making skills.
- Increased financial knowledge isn't just for certain categories of people. We all have unique goals that require unique financial education and knowledge.
- We are all human and are all susceptible to procrastination.
- It is difficult to determine which financial professionals are the dishonest few.
- As we age, personal finance becomes more complex.
- Having accountability drastically increases success rates.

Personal financial planning is one of the most important areas in our lives to focus on and understand; yet we procrastinate, allow the media to drive our emotions, and ask for advice in the wrong places. It is time to put an established system into place that will help to address each category listed above and put a plan of action in front of us that invites individual progress. This system can help individual families make better decisions with regard to their *unique* concerns and needs, and is provided in full detail throughout this book. Make Your Money Work will show you how to implement this established system, whether it is for a company, a non-profit organization, a governmental group, or even a social group. Making your money work isn't just about improving personal finances; it's about improving entire organizations, growing wealth, creating happier families, and living the best life you can with the money you have.

CHAPTER 2:

MAKING THE CASE FOR WORKPLACE EDUCATION

> *"Providing financial education at the workplace is good for the bottom line."*
>
> – Kelly Edmiston, Economist,
> Federal Reserve Bank of Kansas City

By now we have fully established why financial education in America is important. Having greater knowledge in general is typically healthy for any society, but possessing this knowledge in areas such as money and finance offers families the ability to make better life-changing decisions.

Currently, there are many avenues for acquiring financial education. We can sign up for classes at a local community college, sit down with some type of professional, buy audio or video self-learning programs, or read finance publications. Each one of these options delivers some element of education, but each one has both strengths and weaknesses.

- Community college classes
    - Strength – These classes provide an academic curriculum of various financial topics and hold the learner accountable to show up for classes after paying a nominal fee.
    - Weakness – Most classes do not teach many real-world techniques that improve personal finances or that help understand the finance industry.

- Consultations with a professional
    - Strength – Education may be customized to the unique needs of the learner. A degreed professional should have both academic and real-world knowledge. Hourly compensated professionals are not motivated to discuss products.
    - Weakness – Hourly compensated professionals may cost $100 to $400 per hour. Professionals that offer education for free may expect to be hired after educational sessions. Not all financial professionals have degrees in finance or business.
- Self-learning programs
    - Strength – These programs offer a wide array of topics that may be learned at varying paces. They also provide a no-pressure approach to learning.
    - Weakness – Costs vary depending on the topic and duration of program. Programs do not offer opportunity to ask unique questions. Accountability may become an impediment to successful learning.
- Publications
    - Strength – Books and magazines are widely available and constantly updated to current times. Publications allow learners to set their own pace.
    - Weakness – Academic books may not offer real-world advice. Many magazines provide over-generalized advice that may be unwise to act upon. Accountability may become an impediment to successful learning.

As you can see, there is no "perfect" method to disseminate financial education. However, there is a method that brings together an ideal combination of each category above. I will be covering that method very soon. Let's first review how most people have learned about money and finance throughout their lives.

In April of 2011, MSN Money polled 8,000 people in an online survey asking them where they go for trust advice[5]. Here are the results:

- 50% (4,047) - Learned on their own "the hard way"
- 24% (1,884) - Parents
- 9% - Books and magazines
- 7% - The internet
- 3% - Friends
- 3% - A financial adviser
- 2% - A teacher
- 2% - TV

Please remember, respondents in this poll are reflecting *back* to determine where they learned about money, as compared to the Chapter 1 poll which asked where they *would* turn for advice about money if they needed help. There are unsurprising similarities. It is obvious that learning "the hard way" on your own through trial and error can cause enormous life setbacks. Even if you are fortunate enough to evade major mistakes, you may have lost years of time working towards a goal in an inefficient manner. For the 24 percent that learned from parents, they may have avoided making the same mistakes their parents made (if they listened), but it is still novice advice unless their parents happen to be financial professionals.

Even I was surprised to see that only 3 percent of respondents learned about money through a professional. In Chapter 1, we

[5] Money Rates column, "Where did you learn to manage your money?" Beth Orenstein, April 18, 2011.

learned about why many Americans shy away from visiting with a professional for education. In addition to those facts discussed earlier, many Americans believe they cannot afford a professional or that they need to accumulate more wealth for a professional to be worthwhile.

As we reviewed earlier, it is obvious that professional, experienced guidance is typically the best way to increase knowledge in the area of personal finance. However, most Americans choose to take a more difficult and less efficient route when seeking advice or learning about money. What if every person in this country decided to change his or her mind about financial education and sought out a professional? Unfortunately, there wouldn't be enough financial professionals to go around, even when you include the non-independent professionals and those that do not have to act in a fiduciary capacity.

As of 2008, there were only 310,000 licensed financial professionals in the US[6]. If the total population in the US is approximately 308 million, this only leaves one advisor for every 993 Americans[7]. If you attended a large university, you probably remember sitting in a lecture class with 100 to 300 other students. Now, just imagine sitting in that classroom with almost 1,000 people to that single instructor. As you can imagine, the quality of education deteriorates rather quickly with groups of this size. However, this also tells us that financial education may be best disseminated in a group setting. After all, it would be impossible to provide high-quality education on a one-on-one basis for all Americans given the limited number of professionals.

So far we have established that financial education in America is direly needed, it needs to come from professional, unbiased sources, and it is best provided in a group setting to maximize

---

6 Reuters, "Ranks of Financial Advisors Shrinking – Study." August 11, 2010. Helen Kearney

7 US 2010 Census, http://2010.census.gov/2010census/popmap

value and delivery. Furthermore, it needs to be a combination of delivery methods that deal with the issues we have found, or what I call the "education encumbrances": cost, accountability, priority, and real-world advice. Too many families believe they do not have the financial means to visit with a professional due to cost. Without a professional involved, we typically do not have someone holding us accountable to work toward goals. Regardless of our financial means, we all fall victim to the same human issues of priority. For the families seeking advice, they often find it in the wrong places – places that lack experienced, real-world advice. These educational encumbrances require something to help us advance beyond them. They require a system that helps us realize our true potential. They also require a sense of association or connection. They require organizations.

What Employees Want

When I mention organizations, I am speaking about groups that have a desire to help people. This includes, but is not limited to, churches, associations, non-profit groups, and, of course, employers. Let's take a closer look at employer groups.

In a 2011 survey completed by Delloite and ISCEBS, 242 employees were asked what their "top five personal challenges" were[8]. Here are the results:

1. My ability to afford retirement, including post-retirement health care
2. The future of my employment security
3. My ability to earn additional rewards
4. The investment performance of my 401(k)
5. My cost of current health care benefits

[8] Deloitte & the International Society of Certified Employee Benefits Specialists, *2011 Top Five Total Rewards Priorities Survey*. January 2011.

The top personal challenges for American workers listed above are all tied to money and personal finance. Although not in the top five, another mentionable personal challenge which arose for many respondents was elder care. Let's look further into these challenges:

- My ability to afford retirement, including post-retirement health care

The key to understanding how one can afford retirement and post-retirement care is to better understand retirement planning as a whole. This involves looking at retirement income sources, inflationary concerns, changes in law, investment planning, and longevity. It also involves understanding the Social Security system and what risks it may be facing in the future.

- The future of my employment security

If the forecast calls for rain and you must be outdoors, it is wise to prepare and bring an umbrella. If employment security is a concern, being prepared for a layoff is wise. Preparation is the key to a successful career transition. For example, what debts should be kept, what insurances may be altered, and where to access reserve savings without severe consequences.

- My ability to earn additional rewards

People ask employers for greater rewards through monetary and non-monetary compensation. This can be through bonuses, raises, greater benefits, or a 401(k) match. Unfortunately, many organizations continue cutting back on these rewards. American families must learn how to protect themselves from economic downturns when these rewards may become scarce – a trend that simply occurs in natural economic cycles.

- The investment performance of my 401(k)

This is one of the most confusing areas for the American public. This need draws to the heart of the matter – greater financial education is crucial. 401(k) plans don't exactly come with the best "instruction manuals," so ongoing education and advice are direly needed to make wise choices. Ongoing changes in law by the Department of Labor further complicate this area. However, 401(k) investment knowledge is just one small subset of an overall complex area of personal financial planning.

- My cost of current health care benefits

Although all of us are at the mercy of elected officials with regard to health care changes, it certainly helps to better understand these changes and how they will affect us. It is rare to find someone outside of the insurance industry that fully understands the health care changes. Not only would education on these changes in law be powerful, knowledge about tax-preferred vehicles would be equally beneficial (health savings accounts, flexible spending accounts, health reimbursement arrangements, etc.).

Every one of these topics is directly related to money and a better understanding of how to deal with them. The elder care concern, which was also a popular challenge found in this survey, can certainly be dealt with through greater education (where to find care, how to cope with aging parents, how Medicaid becomes available). If these are the top concerns that the average American worker has, then why isn't corporate America responding to them?

Many organizations are trying to respond, but are doing so in ways that do not promote long-term changes in *behavior*. The organizations that are trying to address these issues are putting new tools and benefits in place, but are lacking a system that properly addresses the vast scope of issues at hand and motivates participants to self-improve. Employers need a system that helps with the "education encumbrances" we identified earlier. Throughout this book, I will be sharing with you how to implement this education system to help your organization address the complex issues Americans are facing.

Financial Education Drives Performance

Although I have found very few organizations that already have *successful* education programs in place, they do exist. Let's review an example of a company that started a financial education program for the first time. We will review the rewards that are provided to both the employees and the organization.

In 1999 a chemical production company completed a study throughout their facilities with an organization called the Association for Financial Counseling and Planning Education. This study was meant to review the effectiveness of workplace financial education amongst their work force. After providing financial education programs to employees, each completed 100 confidential surveys. Below are the personal financial behavior changes of the workshop participants[9]:

- 74% - Felt they made better financial decisions since the workshop.
- 75% - Felt more confident making investment decisions because of the workshop.
- 70% - Changed their investment strategies [in 401(k) plan, IRAs, etc.] by diversifying.
- 45% - Increased their retirement contribution amounts.
- 34% - Started contributing to the 401(k) retirement plan.

Through this study, a series of four separate classes were offered to employees by the employer. The topics of these classes varied

---

9 Financial Counseling and Planning, Volume 10 (1), 1999 - Association for Financial Counseling and Planning Education. *Workplace Financial Education Improves Personal Financial Wellness* - www.faircredit.org/files/56.pdf

from the basics of money management to comprehensive retirement planning. The results were very positive with the majority of employees making strides toward their own personal financial goals. The study even concluded that, over an extended period of time, the employees that attended the educational classes reported better overall mental and physical health.

As we have reviewed, money is involved in almost everything we do. Elevating one's knowledge in personal financial planning should therefore help them organize their lives more effectively. In turn, as these studies have shown, they should be more satisfied with the goals they have established in life. Just as many employers focus on helping employees become healthier, better leaders, and more efficient at work, it makes sense to help them improve in an area that is so deeply engrained in their lives. It is all about driving performance.

The benefits to employees have been clearly defined, but what about the performance benefits to employers or other organizations? Employees that are provided educational finance classes that help their long-term futures feel that their employer truly cares about them. It creates a "paternalistic" feeling between employer and employee. Employees that have participated in numerous programs have increased productivity, have less financial stress, take fewer days off of work, and even rate their bosses higher on performance reviews. When an organization provides a program that is directed at helping the employee, not just the company, this resonates with the work force.

In 1998, a Virginia Tech professor by the name of E. Thomas Garman completed an extensive study on personal finances and worker productivity. In his research, he determined that an employer may receive a return on investment between 300 percent and 900 percent depending on many factors of the education program[10]. According to Garman, this return on investment stems from:

- Increased job productivity
- Reduced finance-related absenteeism
- Reduced administrative expenses on transactions such as 401(k) loans and payroll advances
- Reduced Social Security payroll taxes
- Decreased financial stress which often leads to stress-related illnesses
- Reduced health care premiums
- Fewer accidents
- Increased utilization and satisfaction with employer fringe benefits
- Reduced turnover
- Reduced human resources administrative costs
- Less pressure to reduce salaries and wages
- Improved morale and loyalty to employer
- Acceleration of worker retirements
- Reduced exposure to future litigation and fiduciary risk

In his study, Garman illustrated a company spending $200,000 for a work force of 1,000 to benefit from a comprehensive financial education program. The return on investment for all areas listed above was $624,250 or a 312 percent return. Furthermore, he compared providing an education program to providing other benefits such as a 401(k) matching contribution, both of which cost the company money. For the same company listed above, if the average salary was $40,000 and the employer provided a 100% match on the first 3 percent of contributions, assuming 70

[10] E. Thomas Garman, Personal Finances and Worker Productivity, volume 2, number 1, June 1998, pp 81-93.

percent of the employees participated in the plan, the cost would amount to $840,000 in one year. The cost of providing the 401(k) match in this example is 320 percent higher than providing a comprehensive financial education program. As you can imagine, most businesses that are not familiar with this study or how financial education programs work likely assume that a 401(k) match is more important for the business. Although a 401(k) match may be regarded as an important benefit to employees, company decisions, whether we like it or not, are often made with a "bottom line" mentality. This study may further justify that the costs, as well as the benefits, of providing a financial education program benefit both the employer and employee.

All non-safeharbor 401(k) plans in the US have nondiscrimination requirements which force a balance between the amounts of money flowing into the 401(k) from highly-compensated employees versus non-highly-compensated employees. There are complex strategies that help the employer maintain this balance, but one of the easiest ways to target this balance is to have more non-highly-compensated employees participate in the 401(k) plan. Having an impactful education program has been proven to increase the participation rates of employees. In turn, highly-compensated employees may be allowed to place more assets into the plan. This may save the owner(s) money on taxes, but can also serve as a tool to better attract or retain top talent.

Let's take a look at a study done in 2008 by three professors from Duke University, the University of Wisconsin at Madison, and Princeton University, called *The Effects of Financial Education in the Workplace*[11]. In this study, employees, both highly-compensated and non-highly-compensated, were found to increase participation in their employer's 401(k) plan when

[11] *The Effects of Financial Education in the Workplace: Evidence from a Survey of Employers*. Patrick J. Bayer, Duke University and NBER, B. Douglas Bernheim, Princeton University and NBER, John Karl Scholz, University of Wisconsin, Madison, and NBER. January 2008. Pp.16 & 40.

education was provided surrounding personal finance and savings for retirement. This study was compared to employer groups that have a 401(k) plan in place, but do not provide any educational programs. The authors of this report state that, "...it is apparent that frequent seminars have a consistently positive and significant effect on participation in self-directed plans." What is most interesting is the fairly significant difference in their findings between educational programs provided "sometimes or rarely" and programs provided "frequently." In this study, the overall employee base increased participation by 1.43 percent, over groups that provide no education, when education was provided "sometimes or rarely." However, when education was provided "frequently," overall participation in the plan increased by 8.17 percent. By providing an *ongoing* program that helps employees, the additional programs increased participation four fold over programs that may consist of just an annual review of the plan.

This study may then suggest that all employees throughout the entire organization need a program that helps them keep personal finance top of mind and invites better progress towards goals. They need an ongoing, professional program that teaches them about more than just a 401(k) plan. In my opinion, this is the reason why the participation rates in the prior study increased by such an amount when additional educational programs were provided to employees. As we learned earlier in this chapter, the "education encumbrances" of cost, accountability, priority, and real-world advice must be addressed to create effective changes in financial behaviors. With this 401(k) participation study, I believe priority and real-world advice played an integral role in changing these behaviors. A good financial professional should easily be able to provide real-world advice to participants when speaking to them in a group setting, but also, participants are constantly being reminded why retirement savings must be a priority. I would even go so far as to say that accountability may have come into play with this study. If employees mentally promised themselves or even the financial professionals that they would increase their 401(k) savings or begin participating in the plan, they likely felt that a deadline was approaching to fulfill this promise before the professional came in for the next program.

Study after study continues to reinforce the benefits of financial education for the American public. We have also seen that this education directly benefits groups such as employers. This education must be able to address the education encumbrance issues we have found, and it must be delivered in a manner that resonates with the audience. I will now share with you how to begin putting this education program into place through a straightforward six step process. With this guidance, you can begin your new program in as little as 30 days depending on the size of your organization and the parties involved.

CHAPTER 3:

STEP 1 – POSITIONING FINANCIAL EDUCATION WITHIN THE ORGANIZATION

> *"The number one problem in today's generation and economy is the lack of financial literacy."*
>
> – Alan Greenspan

CHAPTER QUICK-VIEW:

- Financial education is best included as a performance and training program, not a wellness initiative.
- It is critical to communicate the correct message to your organization at the launch of your program.
- It is easy to accidently discriminate against certain groups of employees or members when implementing your program.

At your organization, you may have some sort of training and education program in place. This training may range from workplace safety to leadership building. If your organization does not have a training program in place, this may be your opportunity to create one with personal finance as the foundation.

Through my years of experience helping organizations with financial education, I find that about half of them include this education in the overall wellness initiative, while the other half categorizes it as employee training and education. In fact, in 2011, I held a small roundtable event for human resources professionals. The goal of this roundtable was to ask for feedback on financial education programs. When asked whether financial education was considered wellness at their organizations, about half of them felt it was, while the others kept it separate from the wellness initiative.

In my professional opinion, I do not recommend including your financial education program within the wellness package or wellness initiative. When most people think of wellness, they think of becoming healthier, both physically and mentally. We discussed in Chapter 1 how poor financial decisions can certainly affect health, so I am not detaching the correlation. The reason I recommend keeping them separate is that many people judge a book by its cover. It is wrong to do, but it happens all of the time.

When I type "financial wellness" into an internet search engine, I find page after page of information on "financial literacy" and "understanding the basics of finance." We have already established why financial literacy and understanding the basics are important, but let's think about what happens when we position financial education as financial literacy within your organization.

Picture yourself promoting your very first financial education program for the organization. You send a flyer out via email to all eligible members or employees. In the title of your email, you put, "new financial wellness initiative." You will likely have many people that are excited or intrigued by the announcement. At the same time, you will have others that disregard it because they feel they don't need to learn how to "get well" on the topic of money. This happens with health-oriented wellness also, especially with men. Many head-strong males will disregard regular visits to a general physician because they don't feel they need it. Some of them may be correct, but most people in this category would likely discover something new about their state of health and how to improve it if they regularly participated in health checkups.

Given the unfortunate human nature of making instant assumptions, I do not recommend positioning your new financial education program within the wellness initiative. Instead, it should be positioned for the exact reason you are putting it into place – to give back to members or employees and to drive performance. Chapter 7 will cover more details into how you may market your new program to your audience. Here are a few ways other organizations have positioned these programs:

- Professional financial education programs
- Expert financial management programs
- Professional financial development initiatives

You will be able to customize your message for your particular organization, but these examples will resonate with your audience much better than financial wellness or financial literacy. Below are two examples that you are welcome to use as a guide for explaining the premise and goal of your new program:

For employer groups:

XYZ Incorporated is excited to announce a new pre-paid program for all employees – the Professional Financial Education Program (PFEP). After extensive research and preparation, we are eager to provide this new development program to all full-time employees as an addition to the existing benefits package. We understand that economic conditions and changing laws create a challenging atmosphere for all employees, so we have arranged for licensed and experienced professionals to help all of us with complex areas of personal financial planning. Please anticipate further information about our program launch in May.

For church groups and other non-profits:

ABC Organization is proud to announce a new program available to all members and their families. This new program is focused on providing education on complex areas of personal finance. We understand that economic conditions and changing laws create a challenging atmosphere for families, so we have arranged for licensed and experienced professionals to lead educational classes on numerous topics of personal financial planning. We are excited to add this professional education to our existing programs which aim to reach out and benefit our community.

I hope this information gives you better insight into how to position these programs. However, we must first work on a crucial step in your new program – the budget. The reason we must first cover the positioning step is to help you understand where this program may best fit within your organization. Unless you are the sole decision maker, you probably need to approach a board or superior with the idea of a financial education program before receiving approval. Hopefully, this first step will help you become better versed in explaining the program. Then, it's time to crunch through the budget.

CHAPTER 4:

STEP 2 – ESTABLISHING A PROGRAM BUDGET

"It's clearly a budget. It's got a lot of numbers in it."

– George W. Bush

CHAPTER QUICK-VIEW:

- The average cost may range from $0 to $100 per employee.
- Focus on the value and investment return, not just the cost.
- Your new financial education program is an investment that, if utilized properly, should yield a return for your organization.

If you have been involved with bringing on a new program at your organization, you know that it can entail tremendous planning, may involve numerous departments or boards, and often revolves around one major factor – the budget. If you are part of a smaller organization, this process will be much quicker. However, regardless of the size of your organization, here are some thoughts which may help you create a budget for your new financial education program.

If you currently have a training and education budget, I recommend making room for your financial education program within that category. This may mean cutting down on certain programs, but hopefully you have now seen why it may be a strong return on investment to simply add to your existing education budget. If you do not have a training and education budget in place, let's first focus on what the program aims to achieve.

I imagine the goal for your program is to drive the individual performance of participants while also driving the performance of the organization. What would you pay to achieve this goal? Some may say it is a priceless goal if achieved, but I don't think your CPA would agree with your putting an infinity sign next to this category in your budget. There is no magic number in this industry which you must pay per participant, but the range of costs that I have seen is from $0 to $200 per person for the entire organization (I will cover the free programs later). Now, I have seen budgets as high as $2,000 per person for professional financial education, but these examples are often for a certain category of employees, such as executives or managers. For now, we are focusing on the overall organization.

Instead of just focusing on cost, we need to focus on value. If you have specific expectations of your new program and you find experienced vendors that promise to deliver on these goals, you may need to take a leap of faith for a year and give them a try, regardless of the asking price (within reason). However, if you find that the vendors who are promising to deliver the type of program you truly want are out of your price range, it may be wise to revise the budget. After all, the studies I have shown you illustrate returns of at least 300 percent since this is such a powerful area of need. If you must adhere to a strict budget, then find the vendor that most closely matches your needs.

I did mention that programs may cost as little as, well, nothing. I will cover this further in Chapter 5, but free programs must be used with caution. Free is rarely completely free. If you are a non-profit organization or a struggling company, this may be your only option to provide this new program. If you already have some type of education program in place, you may simply include this new free program into the existing one. If you do not have a training program in place, the free option may cost you a minimal amount to establish and implement.

Although it may be tempting to utilize a free program, I typically recommend using a fee-based program. The costs for your new education program are different than the costs for other types of benefits. For example, if you are an employer and pay $2,000 per employee for individual health insurance, you may not receive $2,000 back as a return on investment. There are certainly benefits to offering a group health insurance plan, such as employee retention and attraction, but a group health plan is almost a necessity for competitive industries. When an employee is looking for a dependable employer, he or she is often seeking good pay, a rewarding position, and a strong health insurance plan. Benefits such as health, life, and disability insurance then become a competitive necessity among corporate America.

Financial education programs are not as common as health insurance plans yet, but they are certainly used by smart, competitive organizations. The reason I am comparing these programs to group health insurance is because the education program is more of a direct investment than insurance benefits. Therefore, as you build your budget, think of this as less of a necessary expense and more of an investment. Businesses purchase new, faster computers to use as an investment to increase efficiency, reduce taxes, and increase sales, just as financial education programs may be used to increase work place performance, increase morale, decrease turnover, reduce taxes, and reduce costs.

Ultimately, the creation of the budget will be vastly different for every group. You may have employees or members in various states, your organization may be growing or shrinking, and you may have different goals in place for your program. Therefore, use my ideas and guidelines to customize a program that fits your organization. Over time, you will be able to discover what doesn't work and what does, as this will guide you to the perfect program that fits your budget.

CHAPTER 5:

STEP 3 – CHOOSING VENDORS

"You only have to do a very few things right in your life so long as you don't do too many things wrong."

– Warren Buffett

CHAPTER QUICK-VIEW:

- Pick a vendor that is or has been in the finance field. It will bring real-life experience to your audience.
- If the vendor's speakers are licensed, check their background on free regulatory websites.
- Test-drive the vendor by requesting to see a live class.

Warren Buffet's quote was appropriate for this chapter because choosing vendors may be the most difficult step in my six step series. These will be the professionals that teach and train your organization, so their expertise, integrity, and delivery will make or break your program. With this guidance, I will help you avoid common mistakes and focus on finding an excellent vendor for your program.

Let's first review the types of vendors that are available to help you provide financial education to employees:

- Publication Vendors – These types of vendors simply provide written articles, worksheets, and do-it-yourself books. Although this may be the least expensive route and may provide real-world advice, they have a huge flaw – the educational encumbrances of accountability and priority. What you need is a program that motivates the audience and holds them accountable for taking action on their new knowledge.

- Online Vendors – These types of vendors are a step up from the publication vendors since they often provide the same written material, but include online tracking software and a series of videos. Online vendors may also have a broad array of topics that may be used to coach participants. However, you must rely on all participants to complete these ongoing programs through self-study outside of work.
- Team Vendors – Vendors in this category often work as a team with other group vendors. For example, payroll providers, employee assistance programs, insurance brokers, and wellness providers may all have some element of financial education as part of their overall services. However, the focus is often on the vendor's services with financial education serving as a "less important" additional service. Team vendors may utilize publications, online vendors, or occasionally full-service vendors. This vendor option may be viable, but it is rare to find organizations that have received the full benefits of a financial education program when it is a side-service of another vendor.
- Full-Service Vendors – These vendors are fully focused on providing a successful financial education program for organizations. They often include written publications, online services, and most importantly, an on-site professional educator to teach on various topics. This is the ideal category of vendor if you are serious about financial education. The costs will greatly vary for these vendors, but you will see the greatest results and return on investment if you pick the right full-service vendor. However, there are sub-categories of full-service vendors that must be reviewed.

- Non-profits – Non-profits can be a great resource for financial education if the right factors are met. There are quite a few non-profit organizations that provide financial education, but many of them only focus on one area of personal financial, such as housing assistance, credit and debt, or basic money management. Also, their on-site educators may not have the real-world experience necessary for delivering the educational experience your participants need. A word of caution must also be made for a new breed of non-profit groups that have started in recent years. They have 501(c)(3) status, but are only operating under the guise of a non-profit because their for-profit practices would decrease their ability to be brought into your organization. Please use caution with this category.
- Academic groups – These professionals are very similar to the non-profit groups, but may be an extension of a university. For some of the same reasons listed above for non-profits, you need to be sure they offer speakers with real-world experience, not just academic knowledge. They must also be able to deliver on timely, complex topics of personal finance and possess an understanding of the ever-changing world of investment products that are being shown to the public.
- Investment firms, banks, and insurance companies – You will find many different programs offered by these institutions. They may be a very viable option for you, but there are many areas to understand first. I have devoted much more information below to help explain this category.

- Workplace education providers – This category combines the benefits of non-profit and academic groups, but should have educators with real-world experience. Also, if their sole purpose is to provide financial education and drive organizational performance, they may have the experience necessary to help you carry out a flawless program. This category of vendor may then come down to the budget.

Let me now help you decode the sub-category above – investment firms, banks, and insurance companies. These groups may be as suitable as the workplace education providers as long as they have ample experience with actual workplace *education*. They must also fit a certain criteria. The greatest issue with these institutions is how confusing it is to understand why types of professionals will be walking in to speak to your audience.

For example, insurance companies often employ agents that have securities registrations, the same registrations that the typical financial advisor would have, which are required by law to be able to practice in the industry. These professionals rarely call themselves insurance agents. Instead, they call themselves financial advisors or even financial planners. However, it is crucial for you to be able to spot a "wolf in sheep's clothing." Although a "financial advisor" that is employed by an insurance company may have real-world experience, numerous licenses and credentials, and great speaking skills, there may be a great risk to your participants. If they decide to visit with this professional one-on-one outside of work and hire them, it is almost impossible to know what the true intentions of these recommendations are for your participants.

The professionals that work for an insurance company often have sales quotas to fill each quarter. Also, they often work on commission by offering people various types of insurance products. I have personally seen countless situations where someone completely trusted the word of an insurance professional before dumping their life savings into insurance products that were not in their best interests whatsoever. One such tactic that I often see is the use of whole life or variable life insurance for a retirement or education savings vehicle. This technically can be used as a savings vehicle for those goals, but so can a 529 college savings plan or a 401(k), both of which may offer greater flexibility and tax advantages. The insurance professional probably received a handsome commission from this transaction and may have even needed to do so to keep his or her job at the company due to quotas. This is a conflict that may easily occur if the wrong person is invited into your organization.

Many insurance professionals find themselves in the difficult position of keeping their jobs through sales quotas and doing the right thing for the client. There are certainly good insurance professionals out there that may do a great job within your financial education program, but it is not worth the risk. Instead, if you want to work with a financial institution, I recommend researching investment firms and banks.

Banks are a strange breed. If they do not have licensed financial professionals to speak to your audience, then they will not be the best fit for your organization. They may have an above-average understanding of money, loans, and bank products, but you need dynamic educators that can speak on various topics that also have real-world *financial planning* experience. There are many banks and credit unions now that do have financial professionals though. If so, you will need to research more about the financial professionals. This research I am going to share with you must also be done with investment firms.

One such area to research for both professional groups is what is called a broker/dealer. A broker/dealer is an organization to which the financial professional likely belongs, or the broker/dealer is actually the employer of the professional. If you are able to find out if the professional has a broker/dealer affiliation, you are able to find out quite a bit about him or her. For example, if you discover that he or she is employed by XYZ broker/dealer, you may research this further online. If you discover that the broker/dealer this professional is employed by also owns its own line of investment products (annuities, mutual funds, etc.), then you need to further question this professional to determine if he or she is independent or not. Independence is an extremely important trait to seek out. Non-independent professionals may have conflicts that need to be disclosed, such as recommending investment products that their employer or broker/dealer owns. Being non-independent also means they may be limited as to what investments and tools they can recommend to the public. Non-independent professionals may be a viable choice, but there are many more issues with which to be concerned.

If you discover that the broker/dealer this professional is affiliated with is 100 percent independent, then you may have found the right group for the job. This doesn't mean they are automatically reputable or ethical; it simply means they likely don't have a proprietary product to push on your audience, don't have a sales quota, and don't have as many conflicts, if any at all. There is also another group of independent financial professionals that aren't affiliated with a broker/dealer. This category of professionals is called a Registered Investment Advisor (RIA). You should be able to tell if a professional belongs to an RIA by researching their website. RIAs are very similar to advisors with independent broker/dealers. The differences are beyond the scope of this book, so just know that there may be slightly different rules or laws that each of these groups must follow.

Since your financial education program may have the best results with an experienced, registered professional, here are free resources available that you may use to research their background:

- www.brokercheck.finra.org – This website is brought to you by FINRA, the Financial Industry Regulatory Authority. FINRA is the largest non-governmental regulator for all securities firms doing business within the U.S.
- www.cfp.net – The CERTIFIED FINANCIAL PLANNER™ or CFP® designation is regarded as the premier mark in the financial planning industry. You may visit this website to check the Certified Financial Planner Board of Standards to determine if professionals have achieved these marks or if they have any regulatory actions on their record with the board.
- www.sec.gov – This is the Securities and Exchange Commission website where you may look up background and personal information for RIAs and many independent advisors affiliated with independent broker/dealers.

Now that you know what to look for in a vendor, let's discuss how to begin searching for one. I first recommend asking your peers or friends for referrals to professionals that provide financial education to organizations like yours. Please remember, though, that they may not know what a true financial education program really is. If they recommend an insurance-based financial professional that has spoken to their organization before, thank them for the reference and just keep looking. If you are able to receive a few referrals, add them to your list of contacts. Then, research online to see if you can find a few more to interview. Once you have a list of at least three good potential vendors, it's time for the interviews. Have them send in information about their firm and why they would be the best fit for your organization. Then, look for key areas, both positive and negative. Here are the objectives and characteristics you are seeking:

- Independent – If they are independent professionals, they do not represent an organization that produces its own investment products (life insurance, mutual funds, annuities, etc.).

- Experienced - If they have little to no public speaking skills, they are out. Even if they are the smartest people on earth, if they can't deliver the message in a manner that your organization will understand, they will not work out.
- Teamwork - Are they willing to work alongside other groups such as 401(k) providers, EAPs, or group benefits providers? If not, this is a negative against them. It is essential that all of your professionals can work together to benefit you and your group.
- Broad topic base - They should be able to speak on the six core areas of personal finance – retirement planning, investments, debt management, education planning, insurance, and estate planning.
- Test drive - See if the vendors will allow you to view a live session of their classes with other organizations. Another option is to view a video of a class to see what it entails. However, the video will not be as powerful as seeing a live class. If you cannot sit in on one of their programs, see if they will offer a sample class to you and a small group of decision makers at your organization. This is the best way to determine if their program will work for your group.
- Price structure - Ideal vendors should be able to be paid a fee for their time and services. If they offer everything for free, ask them why they are willing to do so. Some vendors may have both a free, limited service available, as well as the full fee-based service.

Let's discuss the compensation structure for your full-service vendor since it will vary greatly among them. If they charge a flat fee, be prepared to pay $50 to 200 per hour of time spent, or a flat fee for a certain audience size. Again, focus on the value and return on investment, not just the cost. If they offer a free program, this is a viable option, but they need to be fully transparent with you.

The free programs offered by practicing professionals do still come at a slight indirect cost. This cost is no longer on your organization though; it's on the audience members that go through the program in the form of prospective clients. If this route is best for your organization, be sure the educators leave the sales pitch out of the program. Instead, they may offer an evaluation form to participants at the end of the class which offers a consultation with the professionals. Be sure to include a line on the evaluation form which states that your organization does not endorse these professional and that all activities performed with them outside of work are at their own discretion. If you choose this option, I recommend personally visiting with the professionals through the complimentary consultation they will be offering to the overall group. You need to complete your due diligence on these professionals on behalf of everyone that may visit them after your first program. This doesn't mean you are personally hiring this professional. You are simply experiencing the same process which your audience members may elect to try.

CHAPTER 6:

STEP 4 – PREPARING YOUR PROGRAM

> *"I would rather entertain and hope that people learned something than educate people and hope they were entertained."*
>
> -Walt Disney

CHAPTER QUICK-VIEW:

- Segmenting your audiences into "novice" and "advanced" groups will improve the quality of education.
- The room setup must be conducive to both learning and teaching.
- Class durations of one to one and one half hours are optimal.

Once you have the vendor picked, it's time to schedule the first class. Now, some vendors will request that you schedule a full series of classes right away. This is a viable option, but you won't know how many to schedule until everyone has experienced at least one class. Most organizations host two to six educational events per year for the entire organization. For larger organizations, you may also want to segment your audiences. Doing so may ensure that no one is "left behind" in a class if he or she doesn't understand the material or keep others from being bored if a topic doesn't apply to them.

There are many ways in which you may segment your audiences. It may be done by topic, age, or financial knowledge. The easiest way to segment your audiences is into two categories - novice and advanced. I have found that tech savvy individuals will not attend optional events if the title sounds too basic (even though they would have learned something). For the novice group, this will ensure they are not confused and frustrated with the subject matter. You wouldn't attempt to sit through an Economics 405 class as a freshman in college, so don't put your audience through an asset allocation class if they don't know what a bond is.

The most difficult part about determining who should be in each group is, well, determining who should be in each group. I have found two methods to make your segmenting process simple. First, try using a brief survey of questions. You don't need to have anyone answer these questions; this will simply give them an idea of which group they may find to be more suitable. Here are examples of the questions I use:

- Do you understand what makes a stock different from a bond?
- Do you occasionally read business or finance publications?
- Do you know what the term "bull market" means?
- Do you know what is your federal income tax bracket?
- Have you invested in mutual funds before?

If your audience member answers yes to three or more of these questions, I recommend putting them in the advanced category. If they answer yes to fewer than three, I recommend the novice category. Again, they will be encouraged to answer these questions on their own and determine the group for which they are best suited. The other method of segmenting your audience may be done by giving examples of advanced topics versus novice topics. Here are the examples I use when helping groups with segmentation:

Novice topics to be addressed:

- What is "good" debt versus "bad" debt?

- What are the differences between a Roth IRA and a Traditional IRA?
- What is a 529 college savings plan and how does it work?
- What is probate court and why do people try to avoid it?

Advanced topics to be addressed:

- Roth IRA conversion strategies
- Asset allocation techniques
- Estate planning strategies
- Long-term care and elder care

This method of segmentation may give your audience members a better sense of which sessions they would enjoy more. Segmentation is all about the quality of education and learning. Being placed in the novice category does not mean you have no financial knowledge, just as being in the advanced session does not mean you are anything close to a professional. Also, the "advanced" topics may still be covered for the novice groups, but taught in a less complicated fashion. A great speaker with experience should easily be able to adapt these programs to the audience's needs.

Another important step in the preparation process is picking a room where you will host your event. It may sound strange, but the room you choose can increase or decrease the success of your program. Is it too small to hold your audience? Is it too large and everyone sits at the back of the room? Is it located next to a heavy equipment room at your company that creates noise? These are important, yet often disregarded details for a successful event.

I once was brought in to speak to an employer group for the first time to teach a "Finance 101" class. They had never hosted such an event for employees before. My staff told them what to expect when I arrived and what we needed for the presentation area. When I arrived, I found that they had no room to host such an event. Instead, we were in the corner of a large manufacturing floor with wooden picnic tables. This was their lunch-break area. I arrived early to set up the "room" and hand out learning materials. I'm glad I arrived early because once the nice person who arranged this event saw that I had a laptop and projector, she realized what my staff meant when they said I would be using PowerPoint. There was no backdrop for which to project the material. Instead, pieces of standard-sized paper were taped together and placed onto the wall for my projector. While we did this, all of the employees were still working on heavy, loud machinery. A bell then rang that signaled the lunch hour had begun. Everyone started walking over to the picnic table corner, and the room started to become quieter. However, there was one machine still running in the back of the large room. It was extremely difficult for me to speak through the noise to all of the employees. This was one of the worst environments in which I was ever asked to speak.

It was obvious that the company did not take financial education seriously. It also appeared they never had a professional come in to educate the work force using PowerPoint. Furthermore, since the event was held during their one hour lunch break, people began to leave the class early to call loved ones before they went back to work. This was a very poor event, and only a few audience members were able to walk away with quality information.

To prepare your room, I recommend finding one that is large enough to hold your audience, but does not have more than 20 percent vacant seats. "Standing room only" may prove that your event is a popular one, but uncomfortable people lose interest quickly no matter what the topic. Be sure that the room is quiet so that everyone may focus on the speaker. Noise disturbances will continue to break the concentration of the speaker and the audience members.

As for the rest of the room setup, most speakers will be using PowerPoint presentations. Therefore, you will need to have this ready for the event. If you have your own equipment, set it up and test it a day prior to your event. From experience, that projector that has been with the company for five years and has worked just fine will probably decide to quit the job on the day of your event. If you do not have your own equipment and the speaker will be bringing it, be sure to give him or her ample room to set up both a projector and laptop on a suitable backdrop. It is also important to have an extension cord ready for the speaker if needed.

As for the proper placement of chairs and tables, I have found classroom style to be the best. If you have separate tables where participants may sit, do not count on them sitting at the table with their backs to the speaker. Don't even assume these seats are available if this applies to you. If you just have chairs, but no tables, be sure to remind your audience to bring something on which they can write, such as a note pad or clip board. The speaker's arrangement should also be conducive to audience participation. Really great speakers will walk among the audience and interact with them. This means you will want that extension cord out of their way as much as possible. Also, allow them enough room to walk *behind* the projector so they do not need to walk in front of the projector screen to interact with audience members. This can be very distracting to the audience. Here is an example diagram of a suitable setup.

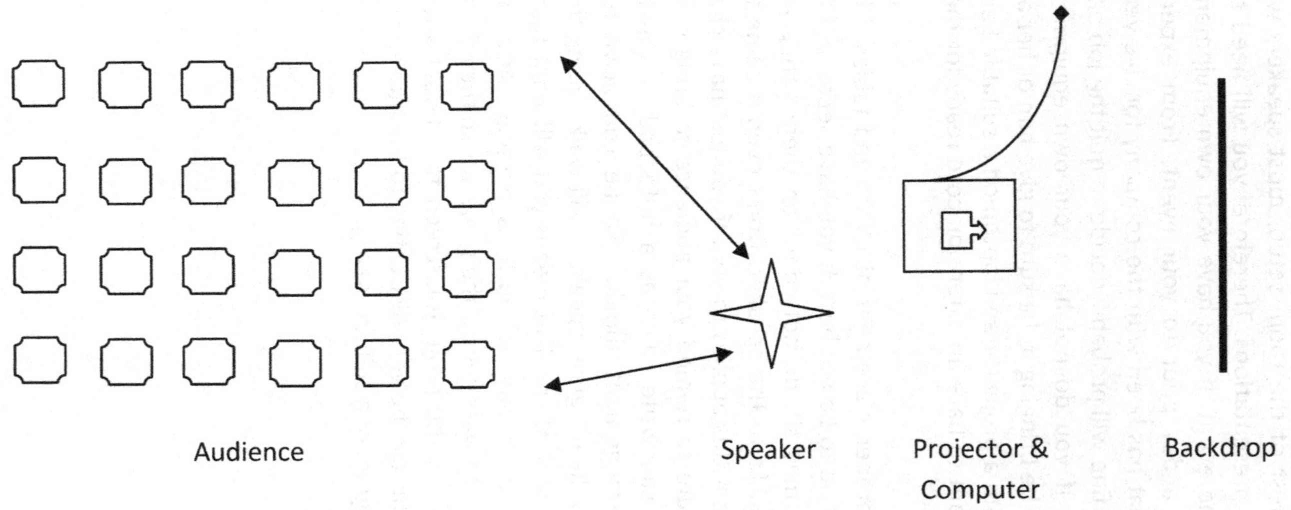
Audience
Speaker
Projector &
Computer
Backdrop

Although rudimentary, there is something to be said about confirming all aspects of the program a day in advance. My staff has always been great about confirming program details both two weeks in advance and a day in advance. However, we are all human. Years ago I was asked to speak to a group of executives and upper management for a very large international company. This audience was obviously a mix of the organization's top talent. Although we confirmed all dates, times, and details as we always do, I somehow had the meeting scheduled 30 minutes later in my calendar than the agreed upon time. Luckily, I had left my office with plenty of time to spare to arrive at the company, but I was extremely rushed to set up the equipment and prepare the room. I was ready just as the audience started walking in the door. This could have turned out to be an embarrassing experience, but was enough to remind me and my staff why we always double-check every detail.

For many of the employers I have helped, they have assumed that the lunch hour is the best time to offer financial education programs. For non-profits and other groups, it tends to be after the normal work day or on weekends. For the employer groups, since the investment and/or time put into this program is expected to yield a return for the organization, I strongly oppose the optional lunch hour programs. For the reasons discussed in earlier chapters, you will not have the attendance you want. Again, you may find that many people judge the book by its cover and will assume they will not benefit from the program. They don't want to sit through a "work function" during their lunch break or they may even be too busy working through the lunch hour to participate. Also, the employees that have no interest in learning about money are likely the exact people you need at the event. Instead, I recommend finding a way to host these events on company time. If you cannot host many of them on company time, I recommend hosting at least the initial classes on company time. This will show your audience just how valuable these classes are and entice them to come to the optional programs throughout the year.

Classes should be one to one-and-one-half-hours in duration. Now, I know what you may be thinking: How can we take everyone off the job for an entire hour and still pay them? Please remember how important this education program is for your organization. This is an investment, just like any other investment in business. You may purchase new technology to speed up communications and cut energy costs. You may also pay for sales or leadership training for employees. Money is a topic that touches everyone at your organization, so it is extremely important to increase the knowledge of how to use it for complex goals.

It is very common to see blood screenings and other health checkups provided by employer groups today. This is because it will help their organization become healthier, prevent illnesses, and decrease health insurance costs. It is much easier to see the return on investment of providing health screenings and checkups because the health insurance premiums are a very transparent cost. It is fairly easy to see when they increase or decrease. However, it is much harder to see the return on investment for a financial education program since the cost savings and benefits come from so many places. Nonetheless, it is just as powerful as providing health screenings. You may be able to keep employees from making horrible financial decisions that will affect their lives, give them insight into their "financial health," and most importantly, drive performance across the organization.

I do realize that many companies are on tight budgets. I also understand that many business owners may find it difficult to measure a return on investment from financial education. If these road blocks are simply immovable, I recommend spending money for just the "key employees" of the business. These are often the professionals that are married to their desks through lunch and operate in "sixth gear" throughout the week. Very often, these employees are putting the company and performance first, and their personal financial goals second. You need a well-balanced key employee group. This may be key salespeople, executives, or any other important position in your organization. It may be easier to imagine spending money on the "key" group for financial education since special benefits are likely already offered to these groups. Once the return on investment is noticed with the "key" group, the free optional programs the rest of the organization is receiving may turn into company-paid time.

CHAPTER 7:

STEP 5 – IMPLEMENTING YOUR PROGRAM SERIES

> *"A person who never made a mistake never tried anything new."*
>
> -Albert Einstein

CHAPTER QUICK-VIEW:

- Positioning your new program with audience members begins with the first announcement.
- Go through the preparation checklist the day before your first event.
- Try bringing in additional speakers for varying topics.
- Focus on ongoing educational support and development to drive performance.

By now you have already established the base of your financial education program. Your vendor has been chosen, the budget is complete, and you are ready to put your new investment to use. It is now time to implement the very first class.

The first step is communicating the new program to your organization. As we discussed in Chapter 1, it is wise not to position this program within the umbrella of wellness. Instead, I recommend positioning it as a professional development program put in place to benefit your audience. This will make the program much more interesting to your group and will emphasize that the program is not about how to help the company; it's about how to help themselves. Here are a few ways you may be able to disseminate your message:

Organization Meeting - Announce the program at a meeting in front of the organization and include a representative from the chosen vendor. This may increase the level of excitement about the program if your audience is able to see you and the vendor announce it. The vendor may also speak about the types of topics that will be covered within the program. I have also seen the meeting option done by video on a company's portal or intranet, if available.

Email – If you must use an email blast, be sure to announce the time and money (if applicable) that your organization spent on bringing the program to the audience. It may also help to have the vendor include a brief bullet-point list of topics and benefits which the program will include. As you know, some people don't always check their email on a regular basis, and if they do, they may not read the entire message. Be sure to use a catchy title to entice everyone to read the message.

Flyers – The least successful way to advertise the new program is by printing out flyers and putting them in hallways or lunch rooms. I have seen this method used by organizations that elect to use free vendors. Unfortunately, they usually have poor attendance at these events and do not enjoy the full benefits of a successful program. Even if a free program is used, every effort should be put forth to make it a success. Flyers simply are not an efficient way of advertising such an important program.

Newsletter – Although better than flyers posted in high-traffic areas, newsletters are an option that may bring about some awareness. However, if this newsletter is five pages long and the new program is mentioned in a small box on the last page, I would not expect to see great results. Instead, if you want great attendance, the new program announcement should be front and center.

Regardless of the medium used to communicate your new program, I recommend highlighting the fact that these programs will not involve any selling. Since your audience members have not been through all of the due diligence that you have been through, they may be skeptical about who is coming to speak to them. If your vendor has been used by multiple organizations, try including this number of prior clients within your advertisement. People want to know that a true expert is coming to educate them, that they will not be pressured into buying something, and that many other people have already enjoyed classes from the chosen vendor. Picture your speaker as a keynote speaker regardless of the size of your group. If you were announcing a keynote speaker, you would be focusing on who the speaker is and how great the program will be.

Once the day of your event arrives, be sure all equipment is working properly (if you are furnishing it), the room has not been double-booked, and all details of the event have been confirmed. Your presenter will likely come early to familiarize himself or herself with the room setup. After your audience members have arrived and you are ready to begin, it is time for you or someone at your organization to introduce the presenter. It is important that the presenter is not asked to introduce himself or herself. The introduction often includes biographical information such as education, background, and skill set. There is nothing more awkward than having to "brag" about yourself in front of a group of people before speaking to them for an hour.

Occasionally, I find myself without someone to introduce me because they are fearful of speaking in front of crowds. When this occurs, I always feel a bit silly telling the group how experienced I am, the amount of education and accreditations I have, and the awards I have received. I might as well be building my own pedestal to climb onto right in front of this crowd of people. Your speaker will appreciate that you don't put them into this situation. What I recommend is having the presenter send you a brief list of bullet-point biographical details that he or she would like to have included in their introduction. This will be much more professional and will help to view this person as an expert on the given topic. In turn, it sets the perfect tone at the start of the program for your audience.

If you belong to a large organization and only one branch or department of the organization is adopting the program, the first event is the best one for others to see firsthand to determine if it would benefit their particular branch or department. This may also be a tremendous benefit to them given that you have already completed all of the research and due diligence on the vendor and the program as a whole. These classes are extremely difficult to describe until you have seen them firsthand. It is like driving a car for the first time. You have seen other people drive before and understand the purpose of the steering wheel, lights, and breaks; but unless you have done it yourself, the experience is nearly impossible to understand.

Your first event is also your opportunity to see what the audience felt about the topic, speaker, handouts, etc. More importantly, this is also your opportunity to discover what topics the audience wants to learn about next. I recommend having a brief survey available at the end of the program which asks what topic should be next in your program series. For example, you could have them rank the following topics from 1-5 depending on their desire to learn more:

- Retirement Planning
- Education Planning
- Debt Management
- Asset Allocation & Investments
- Estate Planning

This information will be important for you to use when scheduling the program series. Each audience is different, so it is difficult to simply schedule each class throughout the year without knowing what your audience finds most interesting. Maybe the audience is relatively young and interested in education planning and debt management. Maybe the audience is more interested in retirement planning. The survey results will help you plan your series of topics and will also make the audience feel more involved in the process.

As discussed earlier, most organizations have two to six programs per year. Your very first event, if the speaker performed well, should create excitement among your group about the program. Grasp this excitement by announcing that additional programs are scheduled throughout the year. Build the expectation that the programs are meant to foster long-term learning and development. If you aren't sure how many events to schedule your first year, try having one per quarter. Then, you should be able to gauge how many events per year are appropriate for your group.

After you have experienced these programs for one or two years, if you have just one speaker presenting on all topics, you may notice similarities among the programs. This may be overlapping material, recycled jokes, or the exposure of a strong opinion over a group of topics. If this occurs, you may want to seek additional speakers. Most vendors will have more than one professional speaker and trainer available. Having new faces speak to your organization may bring new perspectives, opinions, and most importantly, new knowledge.

There are a number of organizations at which I have taught classes, and have done so for many years. Over the course of those years, I went through almost all of my available programs and even repeated a few since laws and markets had changed. Once this occurred, I began offering organizations additional speakers such as estate attorneys and CPAs that I had worked with. These professionals spoke on their respective topics and were able to bring new insights to the audience that I was unable to deliver since I must speak on such a broad array of topics. The only downside to this was that these professionals usually didn't have much speaking experience. Some of them were extremely intelligent, but were difficult to understand or just plain boring. Therefore, I often accompanied them to interject on certain topics and to lead the program.

Regardless of how well your speakers present and teach, it can still be difficult to entice the audience members to change their financial habits and make wise financial decisions each day of the year. As discussed in Chapter 1, people are much more likely to stay on track for goals when they have someone holding them accountable. I gave the example of the success rate of new work-out plans when working with a professional trainer versus being left to our own devices. Obviously, people are much more likely to succeed when someone is guiding them through each step. Your financial education class series will act as this guide in two ways.

First, it is crucial that you continue to host events on a regular, ongoing basis. If you simply schedule classes as-needed when issues arise or when the economy struggles, you are guilty of being reactive. Instead, it is very important to be proactive and provide this education even when you believe it may not be necessary. I have seen this issue with employer groups. They host one event because they want to give it a try and find that it is well received by the entire organization. Eventually, they host another event with a new topic a few months later. Then, the owners or managers that are in charge of scheduling these types of events become busy and allow the momentum to cease. Eventually, many months have gone by and they start forgetting just how powerful the programs were when they were implemented. Please remember that you may become busy and feel the need to put work-related items on the "back burner," but at the same time, someone at your organization may be going through a horrible divorce, grieving over the loss of a close family member, or stressing over how to pay for the college their twins are attending next year. Being proactive in scheduling your ongoing program will help to ensure no one is put onto *your* backburner.

Second, hopefully you have found a vendor that provides further education and guidance outside of the "classroom." If you are hosting only four events per year and each event lasts only one hour, this leaves a tremendous amount of time for the audience member to lose momentum. Below are examples of outside services that may work well for your audience:

- Workbooks – Although it may bring back nightmares from burying your head in a textbook, workbooks can be a great way for the audience to track progress towards goals. This may be a savings goal or even a checklist of to-do items. Workbooks are most often used for novice groups.
- Computer Programs – This category may allow the audience to track the same goals as listed in the workbook section, but can include automatic reminders, email alerts, and helpful progress charts.
- Newsletters & Articles – These educational pieces are great to send out with timely tips and topics. They may also include real-life stories to which audiences can relate.
- Phone Time – Some vendors will allow a limited amount of time for the audience to speak with them by phone in between programs. This may range from a 1-800 call center number to the actual presenter accepting calls with financial questions and concerns.
- Personal Consultations – This option is most common when your vendor is a practicing professional. We already discussed what precautions may be taken with this type of vendor. However, as long as you have hired an independent professional who isn't pitching products, the

personal consultations are often the most valuable and effective outside service.

The other benefit to having regular, ongoing education is that programs will continue to be updated to the current laws, markets, and economic environment, assuming your vendor has the same philosophy. At the beginning of this book, we reviewed many major world economic events that have occurred since the year 2000. Financial education programs from 2002 look much different than they do today. If it seems your vendor is not keeping up with changing times, I recommend encouraging them to do so.

Once you have begun your financial education series and provided ways to encourage wise decisions, it is time to track and monitor progress. This can be one of the hardest parts of the process, but I will share with you a few ways other organizations have done so.

CHAPTER 8:

STEP 6 – RETURN ON INVESTMENT

"There are many ways of going forward, but only one way of standing still."

-Franklin D. Roosevelt

CHAPTER QUICK-VIEW:

- Create a formal progress review after one year of implementation.
- Measure absenteeism, utilization of fringe benefits (tax savings), morale, and productivity.
- Use surveys if you are unable to complete a formal review.

The final step is to measure the return on your investment. This is an extremely hard step in the process since many factors do not have easily attainable numbers. These factors include those listed in Chapter 2, such as greater worker productivity, reduced turnover, and accelerated worker retirements. Having a complete performance or progress review will allow you to gauge the success of your program and determine how to best adapt it to your organization moving forward. The review process is most beneficial for companies. If you are in the corporate world and have decided to pay a fee for a financial education program, there are probably others in the company who are very interested in seeing the progress of the "new expense."

The best time to complete your first formal performance review is after implementing the program for one year. Please note that there are areas of performance that will be very difficult to gauge after just one year. The one-year mark is simply the beginning of your performance review process. It will allow you to take measurements on certain areas of improvement that will be helpful in completing deeper reviews in years to come. Your initial review will serve as the "foundation." The one year areas you may be able to measure are productivity, absenteeism, payroll taxes, utilization of fringe benefits, and morale. If your organization does not have systems in place to measure these areas, here are some basic ideas to help you begin the process:

Productivity – Productivity is a very broad category, but most organizations are likely to focus on the return on investment (ROI) to measure performance. When measuring ROI, use quantifiable factors to build your calculation. For example, this may be measured in additional units sold over a certain period of time for a sales team, a decrease in the number of defective production units, increased response times, or a decrease in the number of accidents. Less quantifiable factors include increased customer satisfaction and increased job satisfaction.

Absenteeism – If your organization has a formal attendance-tracking system in place, monitoring absenteeism improvement should be very simple. If your organization does not, then split this task into departments for easier tracking. Absenteeism should also be split into two categories – planned and unplanned. Both categories can be costly to an organization, but unplanned absences are much more expensive due to their effects on productivity, work quality, and morale.

Payroll Taxes & Utilization of Fringe Benefits – These two categories are directly tied together. If your education program is succeeding, the increased utilization of certain fringe benefits should help to decrease payroll taxes. Start with the fringe benefits by looking at enrollments and usage of all benefits. In particular, pay close attention to benefits such as Section 125 cafeteria plans and pretax insurance benefits, as these benefits may decrease payroll taxes for the organization. An accounting professional should easily be able to provide you with a hard number for your review. If your organization does not have these benefits, I recommend speaking with someone about how they may benefit your group. Increases in utilization for all benefits in an organization, even those without a tax benefit, should improve job satisfaction, accelerate retirements, and increase productivity.

<u>Morale</u> – Although morale may seem difficult to quantify, it can be done very easily by surveying the very people you are trying to help. If you already have a morale survey in place, this will help to quantify improvement over the time prior to your education program. If you do not have a morale survey in place, this will provide a comparison point for the future and reveal current morale. You may ask a question such as "Do you feel like an important part of your organization?" or "Do you feel that your personal development is important to your organization?" Morale is very likely to improve with the introduction of a good financial education program.

Productivity, absenteeism, and decreased payroll taxes (by way of utilizing fringe benefits) are all factors that may easily have a dollar value next to their improvement. However, morale is different. The difficult factor with morale is putting a dollar value on a *feeling*. You must ask yourself, "How much value do we place on making our work force happier?" From experience, organizations that have happy, satisfied, and engaged work forces are typically more successful. I'm sure you have heard the adage, "The No. 1 asset in any organization is the people." Happy, engaged work forces drive themselves to improve and grow the organization. This, whether consciously or unconsciously, resonates with consumers.

Hopefully, you will see obvious improvement in the performance of your work force after your program has been in place for one year. The categories above should help you determine your actual return on investment. Then, you will need to determine which areas require the greatest focus for the next year. If your organization has seen a quantified positive return on the time and money spent on your program, it is a success! Hopefully, this return is at least 25 percent. In the examples provided in Chapter 2 by Virginia Tech, your return on investment could be as high as 900 percent when including all of the positive factors listed in the study.

If you are not satisfied with the program, evaluate all of its parts once again. Review the information provided in Steps 3 and 5. Maybe there is room for improvement in the implementation process. Maybe you could try a different vendor. If you used a "free" program, you didn't have a true cost besides the time spent deploying the program. Even so, you are still able to calculate your return. I have seen much greater returns and success rates for programs that come at a fee as compared to "free" programs. If you were not happy with your free financial education program, try using a vendor that charges a fee. That fee will typically bring you better speakers, better material, and more engaged participants.

If you don't feel the need to complete the entire review process, you may simply use a survey that asks your audience members if the program has helped them. These example questions include:

- Have you utilized the information given to you during the professional financial education program (PFEP)?
- Do you feel the PFEP has helped you build financial goals and/or work toward those goals?
- Do you feel the information in the PFEP pertains to you and your needs?
- Would you like to continue receiving PFEP classes?

At the very least, this simple evaluation should give you an idea of the value in the eyes of the audience. It will not provide you with hard numbers for analysis, but it may be enough to justify discontinuing or continuing the program.

I have been a guest at many types of organizations to help them with financial education programs. It is surprising to me just how different some organizational cultures really are from group to group. Some of the more successful organizations I have helped are fully engaged in their work force and try very hard to help each person with personal development. From these organizations, I found a few new ideas I will share with you.

First, it is no surprise that rewarding groups with free food (usually lunch) for attending an education program will draw greater crowds. I have seen this tactic work best with organizations that prefer to use free vendors rather than paying a flat fee. These organizations usually don't allow people to attend the programs on company time, so the attendance may sometimes be low. This is especially true on Fridays at lunch when the weather is nice outside. To entice and reward your audience members, at least offer them lunch for attending. This will help the program become more successful.

Second, if you have people at your organization who have seen great personal success by utilizing the knowledge provided within your education program, ask them if they would be willing to write a few brief sentences about why they have benefited from it. With their permission, this may be shared in a newsletter or flyer to show that the programs really work. Then, reward those people for offering their feedback.

Third, offer incentives for completing an entire program series. Over the course of a year, if you host six education programs, all of which cover different financial topics, this series likely covered a broad array of great information. If your audience members took the time to work through all of the programs, reward them with a gift card, food, or a giveaway. I have commonly seen organizations put their names into a hat for a free gift card or an MP3 player.

Fourth, a less common, but innovative idea is using the progress and attendance of your education program during employee review meetings. If employees have been dedicated to learning and self-improvement through your education program, they are likely also focusing more on their careers. Again, better personal performance will drive organizational performance. This behavior should be rewarded during regular reviews.

As I have stated earlier, the most innovative and successful organizations I have helped are engaging in financial education programs and other development endeavors. Not every organization is following suit. Some organizations simply don't want to "waste the time and money" on providing development programs to the work force. However, the "smart" organizations that do so should brag about it! Use this benefit as a recruiting tool, especially if you are paying a fee for a program. Trust me, this will set you apart from many other competing organizations.

One of the best ways to brag about your program is by issuing a press release. If you are with a large organization, you have likely issued press releases before. If you haven't tested the waters with press releases before, give a call to a local public relations (PR) firm or a public relations website. PR firms will be more expensive for press releases, but they will be able to help you customize your message and utilize search-engine optimization strategies. The PR websites are cheaper, but may simply be dumping your press release out into the web without any guidance. Below is an example of a press release you may issue regarding your successful financial education program:

For Immediate Release

XYZ, Inc. Focuses on Employees – New financial education program drives success

Anywhere, USA – XYZ, Inc. has announced the implementation of a new program focused on helping the work force become healthier and wealthier. This new program delivers timely financial education and training to help organization members stay on track for important life goals. With the help of ABC Financial Education Partners, XYZ, Inc. is able to provide renowned industry experts to facilitate these programs.

"We truly care about the personal development of our work force and know that personal finance can be a very complex and daunting topic," says John Johnson, President of XYZ, Inc. "The average American family spends more time planning its annual vacation than they do their personal finances. This will help all of us make personal finance a priority."

XYZ, Inc. produces widgets and was founded in Anywhere, USA…… (Insert organization info here)

I have one more tip to give you regarding your press release. If you do include the names of the vendors you are using, they are benefiting as well since they are also receiving recognition through the press release. Therefore, ask if they are willing to cover the cost of the press release. You may even split the cost with them if you wish. I have found that many vendors are more than willing to support joint marketing ideas such as this.

CHAPTER 9:

BRINGING IT ALL TOGETHER

By now, you have all of the information you will need to begin a very successful financial education program. It is essential that you keep the end-game in mind from the very beginning. If implemented properly, your financial education program will provide meaningful and actionable education to your audience while driving greater organizational performance. Here are my final recommendations to keep in mind as you begin your program:

- If you are part of a large organization, especially one with a tight budget, and must convince your peers that this endeavor is needed, it is crucial to stress the importance of this new program on the bottom line. The difficult economic times will help you to justify why it is essential to join the bandwagon of organizations that are already helping their work force.
- Financial education must be seen by all audience members as a valuable perk, not an obligatory program that just helps the organization. It must also be seen as advanced and professional. If you simply stress this new program as a budgeting and debt-planning class series, your more tech-savvy members will ignore it. Budgeting and debt planning are very important topics to be covered, but you cannot discriminate against the audience members that need advanced financial planning guidance. As we discussed, the advanced learners and "key" members of your organization are likely

overwhelmed by the myriad of financial issues they must address as compared to the "rank and file."

- If you have assets available in your budget to pay for your new financial education program, I recommend paying some sort of fee. This does not mean that free vendors are a bad choice; this will simply remove the salespeople from your vendor list since they may not be interested in providing ongoing education – they want a group of live prospects.
- Regardless of which type of vendor you pick (free or fee), I recommend using a licensed and experienced professional. These experts are likely able to handle basic as well as advanced topics. Non-licensed or academic-education providers typically do not have the professional experience of working with live, complex financial planning issues. Your "key" member groups will especially need educators that are equipped with this knowledge.
- To adequately prepare for your program, review all steps listed in Chapter 6. Too many times I have become a victim of an organization's lack of preparation when visiting them to teach classes. This will prove to your organization that this is a professional program and has been done in a professional manner.
- If you are in the corporate world, I highly recommend using company-paid time for your education program. You will experience the best results this way.
- The presenters are the key to your education program. They may have the best material in the entire country from which they are teaching, but if they are unable to really connect with your audience and inspire them to focus on their long-term goals, you will not experience your intended results.

- Accountability and one-on-one guidance will help to drive success in your program. It is important for the vendors to have off-site assistance available to all members of your audience. This will also help to ensure ongoing support is made available to increase the likelihood of achieving long-term goals.
- Continue to survey the audience during the education process and at progress points. It may seem like a daunting task, but this feedback can be very powerful when used to fine-tune your program.
- Brag about your new financial education effort! Even from the onset of the program, you have bragging rights. Use the press release, brag about the organization spending resources to bring the program to the audience, and utilize this as part of your recruiting effort.

If you have made it this far in the book, you can likely tell that I am very passionate about bringing financial education to the American public. This body of knowledge is so crucial to our lives, yet it is distorted with salespeople and a myriad of complex subsets that have yet to become a true focal point in our education system. Health and wellness are areas that most Americans realize are important; yet we have the largest percentage of obese citizens in the world living here. Ironically, stress about money and personal finance leads to even poorer health.

Financial education has countless benefits for the average American. It can change the lives of a family for generations to come. If financial knowledge is instilled in a young couple at the onset of their marriage and they are motivated to make wise financial decisions together, they are much more likely to have greater wealth, be healthier, have a happier marriage, have less stress, and provide a better lifestyle for their children. Just imagine if this young couple purchased a home that was within the means of their budget and still kept enough money each month to set aside for a child's college and their own retirement. As their child grows, they continue to save toward these goals and live within their means. When they have emergencies that arise, they use funds from their emergency fund. They send their child off to college and pay for 75 percent of tuition. They haven't set their retirement goals back with the burden of student loans since they saved early for both college and retirement. They eventually retire with sufficient assets to life a comfortable, modest lifestyle – the lifestyle they desire. Along the way, their children see how they have lived successful lives and learn from them how to save, set goals, and make finance a priority.

This family continued focusing on their long-term goals and was able to achieve them because they had the drive and knowledge to do so. Yes, there may be divorces, deaths, and health issues along the way that no one can truly plan for. However, even a family that plans for the best and is dealt the worst will be better positioned to recover from such unfortunate shortcomings. My own family may serve as an example.

I often wonder what my life would be like if better financial decisions had been made during my childhood. Now, I have no desire to change the course of history, nor do I desire to change the present. My entire family is very happy today, and my wife and I live the lifestyle we desire. In fact, I feel that the financially desolate years we lived through helped to mold my desire to help people with money. This hard work and sacrifice shared among my family built character in all of us. I simply reflect back on those days to analyze what may have been done differently were financial education a part of my parents' lives.

I imagine that my mother would have run her business more efficiently if greater financial knowledge had been instilled. This may have helped them cut costs and increase profits. More income may have been set aside for college for my brother and me if efficient tax-planning methods and college calculations had been introduced to them. They may not have struggled trying to reestablish college savings the years prior to my freshman year (after being used on the long, expensive divorce). This may have allowed them to focus on debt payments or even retirement savings instead of making up for lost time and lost assets. Making wiser financial decisions certainly would have saved everyone great stress and mental hardship since financial issues were the root of most of our problems. Time has yet to tell if these depressing years took a toll on the long-term health of my family.

There is no way to tell what may have changed if greater financial knowledge had been a part of our family history. Everyone reading this book likely has a story of hardship that may have been altered if greater knowledge had been available to navigate the difficult financial decisions that arise in life. Financial knowledge will not help every single person in this country, nor will it change unbreakable behaviors. However, I am confident that by spreading this education to the average American family, we will have a happier, healthier, and wealthier society. This knowledge does not come from our education system. This knowledge must come from the organizations and companies to which we all belong – the groups that have a beneficial interest in changing the lives of the American families they touch each and every day. In turn, they themselves will enjoy healthier and more profitable work forces and will become the drivers of a greater society for generations to come.

Made in the USA
Monee, IL
04 November 2026

67378684R00049